Book and CD

Really Easy Guitar

T0048189

Scales

Wise Publications
London/New York/Paris/Sydney/Copenhagen/Berlin/Madrid/Tokyo

Contents

Published by
Wise Publications
14-15 Berners Street, London W1T 3LJ, UK.

Exclusive Distributors:
Music Sales Limited
Distribution Centre, Newmarket Road,
Bury St Edmunds, Suffolk IP33 3YB, UK.
Music Sales Corporation
257 Park Avenue South, New York, NY 10010,
United States of America.
Music Sales Pty Limited
20 Resolution Drive, Caringbah,
NSW 2229, Australia.

Order No. AM972543
ISBN: 0-7119-9175-8
This book © Copyright 2004 by Wise Publications

Unauthorised reproduction of any part of this
publication by any means including photocopying
is an infringement of copyright.

Written and arranged by Cliff Douse
Edited by Sorcha Armstrong
Music processed by Simon Troup
Book design by Chloë Alexander
Photographs by George Taylor
Printed in Great Britain

CD mastered by Jonas Persson
Guitars by Arthur Dick

Your Guarantee of Quality
As publishers, we strive to produce every book
to the highest commercial standards.
The music has been freshly engraved and the
book has been carefully designed to minimise
awkward page turns and to make playing from it
a real pleasure.
Particular care has been given to specifying acid-
free, neutral-sized paper made from pulps which
have not been elemental chlorine bleached. This
pulp is from farmed sustainable forests and was
produced with special regard for the environment.
Throughout, the printing and binding have been
planned to ensure a sturdy, attractive publication
which should give years of enjoyment.
If your copy fails to meet our high standards,
please inform us and we will gladly replace it.

www.musicsales.com

Got any comments?
e-mail reallyeasyguitar@musicsales.co.uk

Introduction

Welcome to the *Really Easy Guitar Scales* book, a useful reference for all guitar players.

This book will show you how to play scales in each of the twelve keys. It also explains the basic theory that determines how the scales are formed.

The accompanying CD features professionally recorded versions of each of the scales in this book so you should listen to these to make sure that you are playing them properly.

Just follow our three step guide to using this book and you will have an extensive knowledge of scales and the theory behind them in next to no time.

Happy music making!

1 Tune Your Guitar

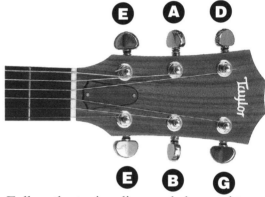

Before you can start to play along with the backing tracks, you'll need to make sure that your guitar is in tune with the CD. Track 1 on the CD gives you notes to tune to for each string, starting with the top E string, and then working downwards.

Alternatively, tune the bottom string first and then tune all the other strings to it.

Follow the tuning diagram below and tune from the bottom string upwards.

6th to 5th string	5th to 4th string	4th to 3rd string	3rd to 2nd string	2nd to 1st string

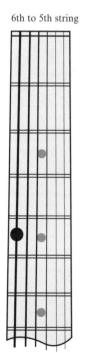  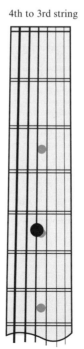  

2 Understanding scales

Scales are groups of notes taken in ascending or descending order of pitch. These can be used to create melodies and solo improvisations.

There are many different scales and each one has its own name and distinct character: the major scale has a nice, melodic sound that you will recognise from many types of upbeat music, while the natural minor scale has a melancholy character that makes it ideal for ballads; the blues scale has a very distinctive sound that reminds you of the type of music it got its name from; and the dorian mode, a more exotic kind of scale, has a much jazzier sound.

Intervals

Each of the notes in the scales listed in this book are separated by intervals. The smallest possible interval between two notes is called a semitone (S) and two semitones make a tone (T). Notes on either side of a guitar fret are separated by a semitone.

E string example

In this example on the E string, A and B♭ are one semitone (fret) apart.
Play the notes at the 5th and 6th frets on the bottom E string and see how they sound.

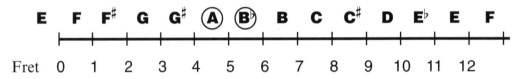

If you move the second note two frets away from the first note instead of just one, the interval between them will now be a tone:

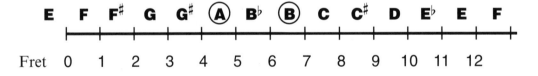

Some scales, such as the pentatonic scales, even have some notes that are a tone and a half (a tone plus a semitone) apart, like this:

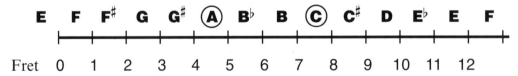

3 Understanding scale patterns

We can also use chord box diagrams to show you certain useful scale patterns on the fretboard. When a box is used to describe a scale pattern, suggested fingerings are also included.

Black circles show you the root note of the scale. If the root note of the scale is an open string, this is indicated by a double circle. In this book, 2 shapes are given for each scale. The first shape is demonstrated on the accompanying CD over two octaves. Grey circles represent notes outside this range.

A Scales

A minor pentatonic

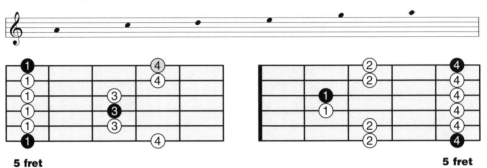

A major pentatonic

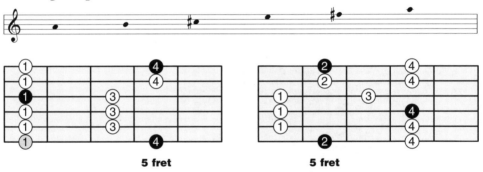

A blues scale

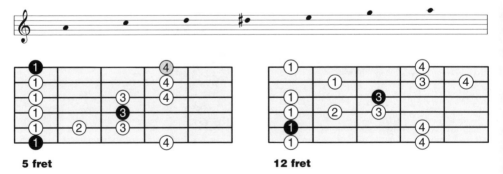

6

A Scales

A country scale

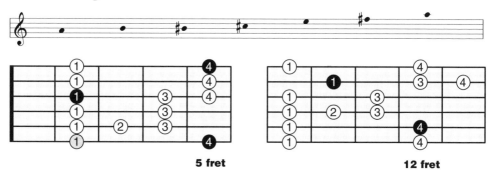

5 fret   12 fret

A major

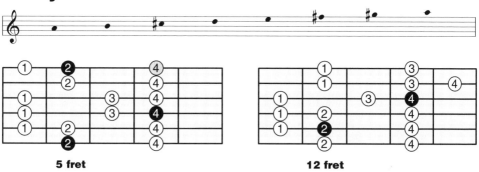

5 fret   12 fret

A natural minor

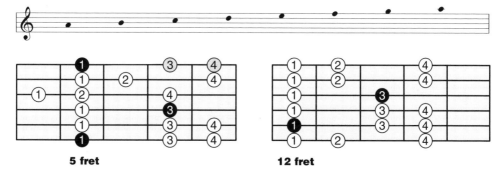

5 fret   12 fret

A melodic minor

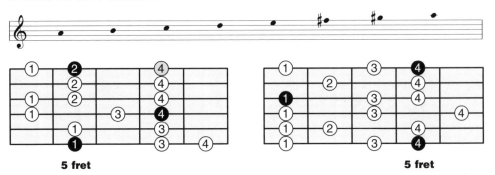

5 fret   5 fret

A harmonic minor

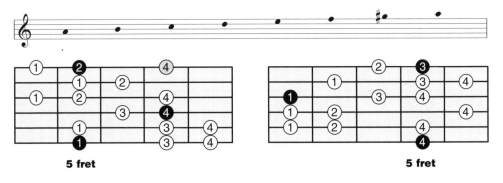

5 fret   5 fret

A dorian

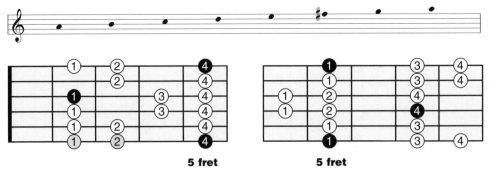

5 fret   5 fret

A Scales

A mixolydian

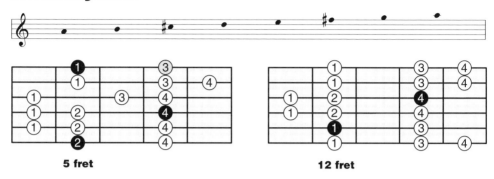

5 fret   **12 fret**

A whole tone

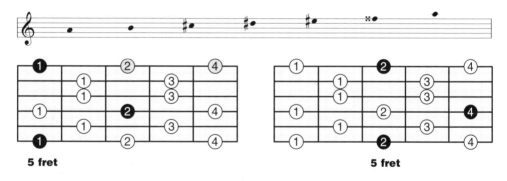

5 fret   **5 fret**

A diminished

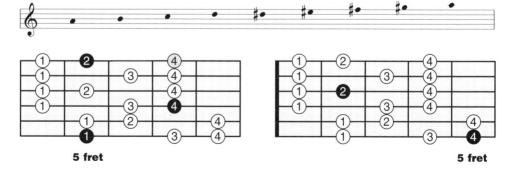

5 fret   **5 fret**

9

Bb (A#) Scales

Bb pentatonic

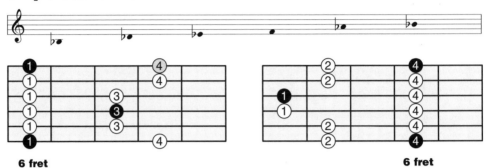

6 fret

6 fret

Bb major pentatonic

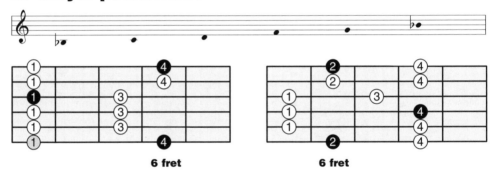

6 fret

6 fret

Bb blues scale

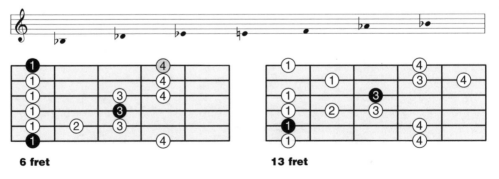

6 fret

13 fret

B♭ country scale

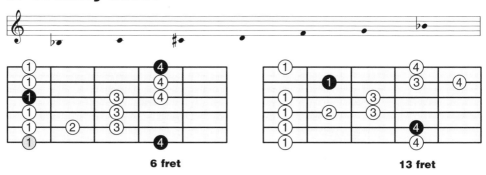

6 fret **13 fret**

B♭ major

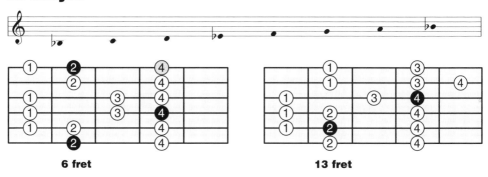

6 fret **13 fret**

B♭ natural minor

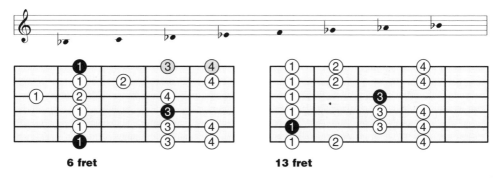

6 fret **13 fret**

B♭ (A♯) Scales

B♭ melodic minor

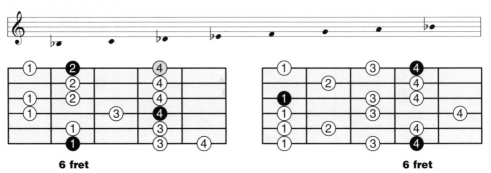

B♭ harmonic minor

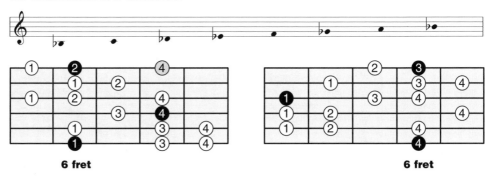

B♭ dorian

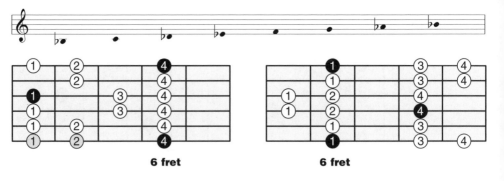

Bb mixolydian

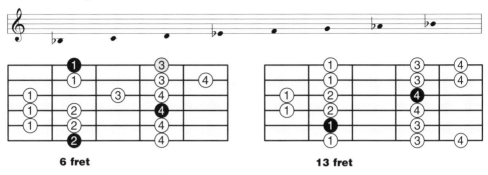

Bb whole tone

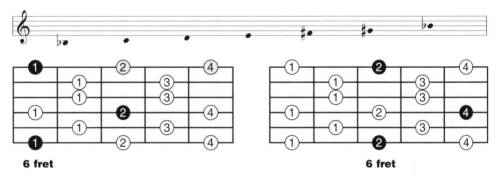

Bb diminished

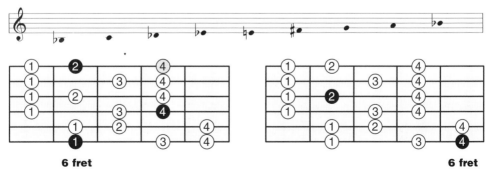

B Scales

B minor pentatonic

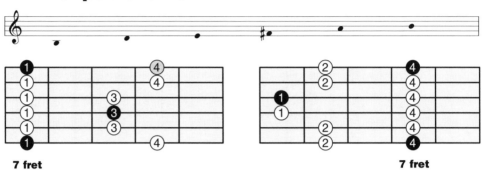

7 fret

7 fret

B major pentatonic

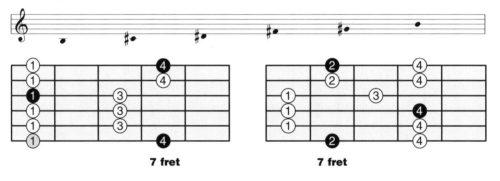

7 fret

7 fret

B blues scale

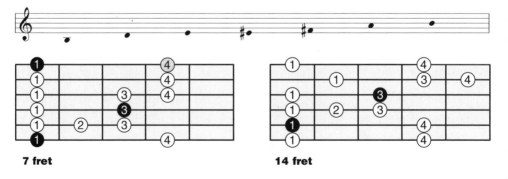

7 fret

14 fret

B Scales

B country scale

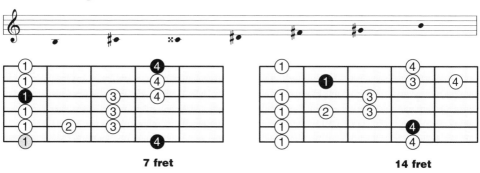

7 fret

14 fret

B major

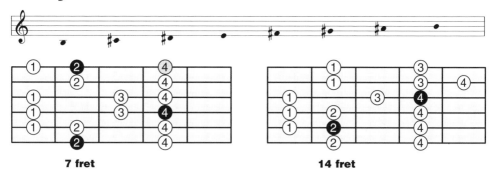

7 fret

14 fret

B natural minor

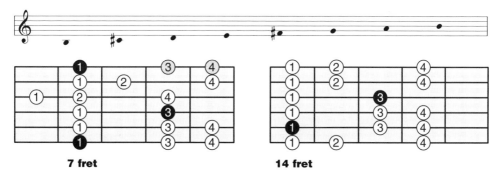

7 fret

14 fret

B Scales

B melodic minor

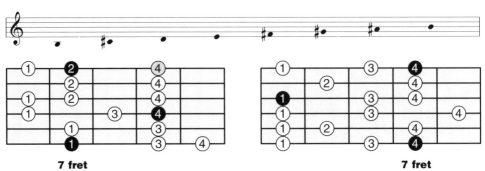

B harmonic minor

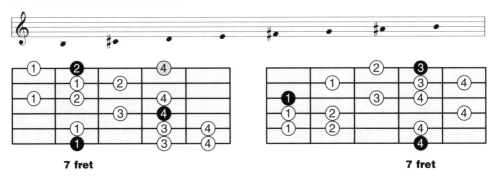

B dorian

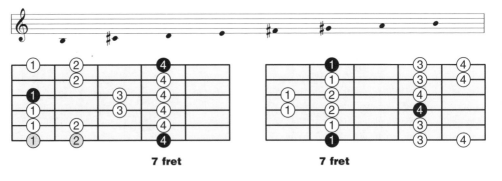

13

B mixolydian

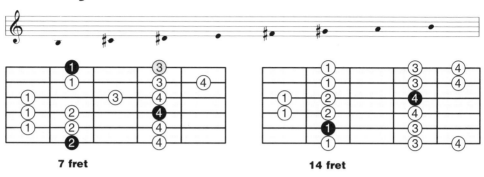

7 fret   14 fret

B whole tone

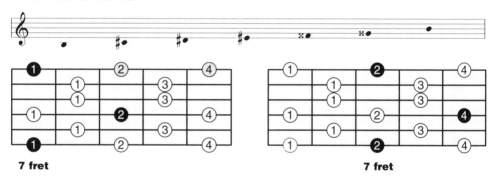

7 fret   7 fret

B diminished

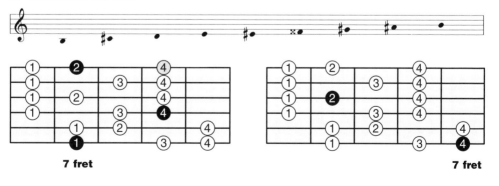

7 fret   7 fret

C Scales

C minor pentatonic

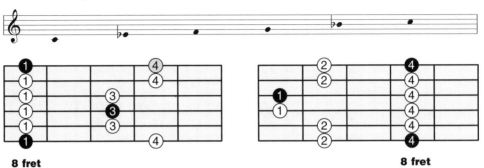

8 fret   8 fret

C major pentatonic

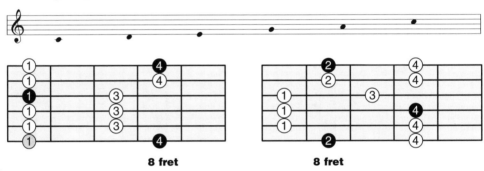

8 fret   8 fret

C blues scale

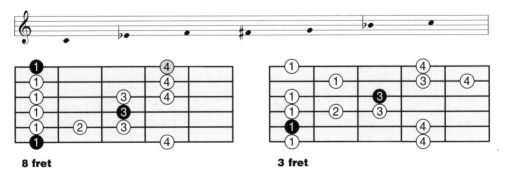

8 fret   3 fret

C Scales

C country scale

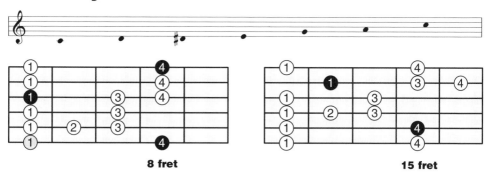

8 fret   **15 fret**

C major

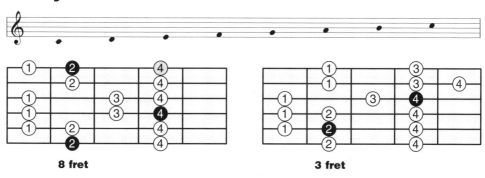

8 fret   **3 fret**

C natural minor

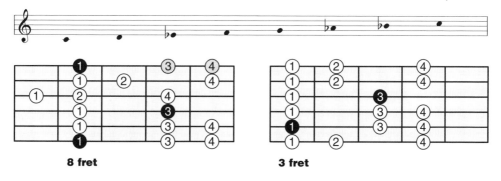

8 fret   **3 fret**

C Scales

C melodic minor

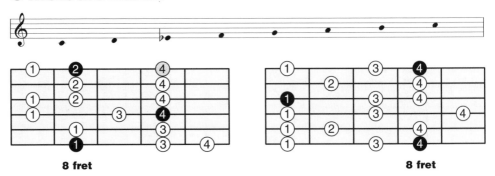

8 fret   **8 fret**

C harmonic minor

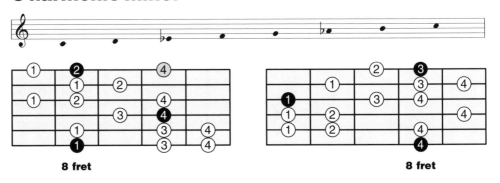

8 fret   **8 fret**

C dorian

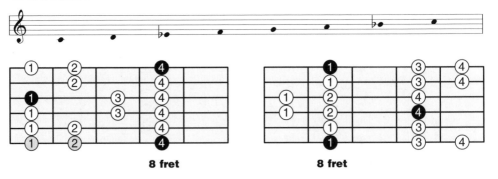

8 fret   **8 fret**

C Scales

17

C mixolydian

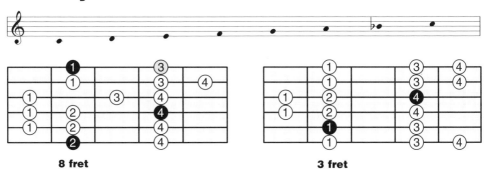

C whole tone

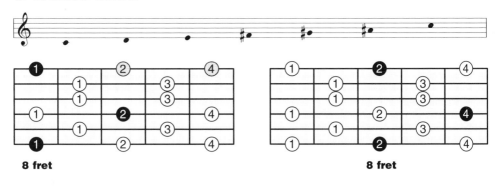

C diminished

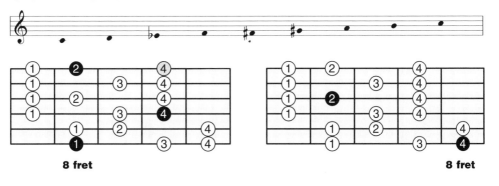

C#/Db Scales

C#minor pentatonic

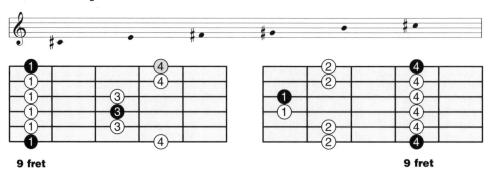

9 fret   9 fret

Db major pentatonic

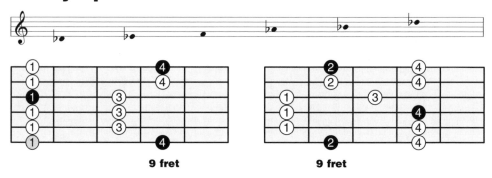

9 fret   9 fret

C# blues scale

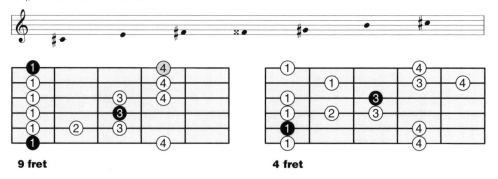

9 fret   4 fret

22

D♭ country scale

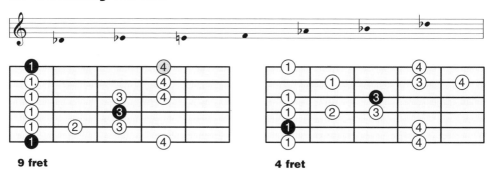

9 fret   **4 fret**

D♭ major

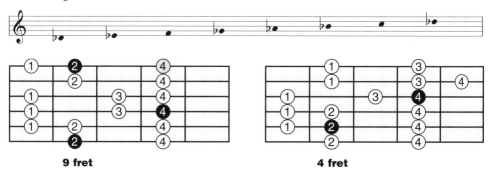

9 fret   **4 fret**

C# natural minor

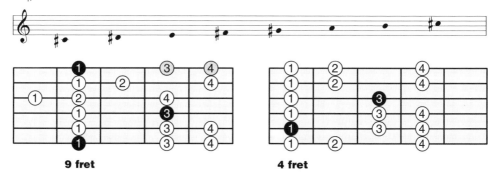

9 fret   **4 fret**

C♯ melodic minor

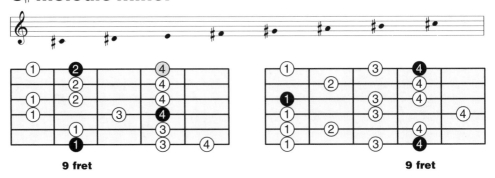

C♯ harmonic minor

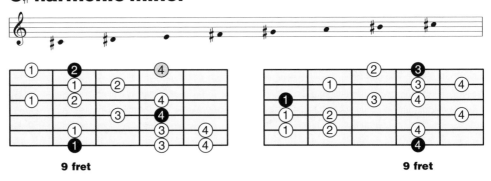

C♯ dorian

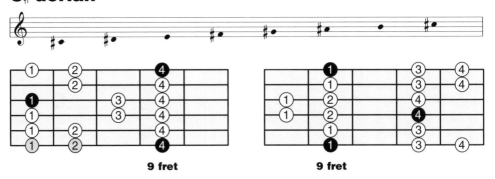

Db mixolydian

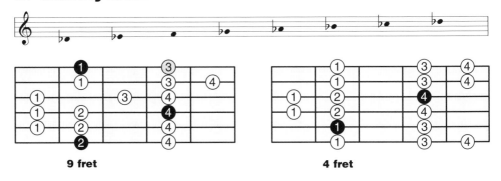

9 fret

4 fret

Db whole tone

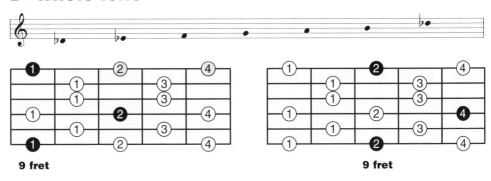

9 fret

9 fret

Db diminished

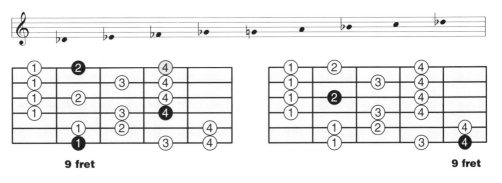

9 fret

9 fret

D Scales

D minor pentatonic

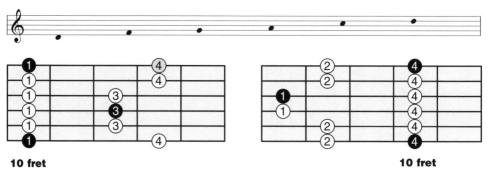

10 fret   10 fret

D major pentatonic

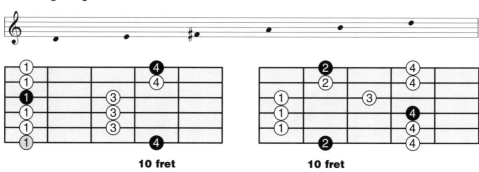

10 fret   10 fret

D blues scale

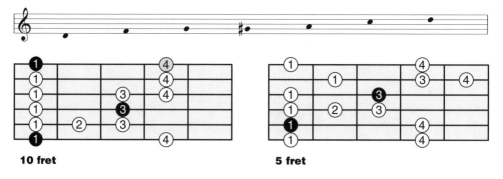

10 fret   5 fret

D country scale

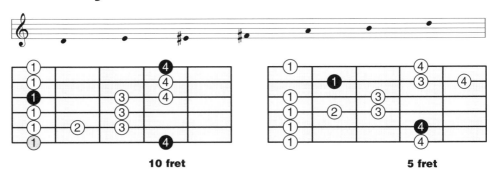

10 fret **5 fret**

D major

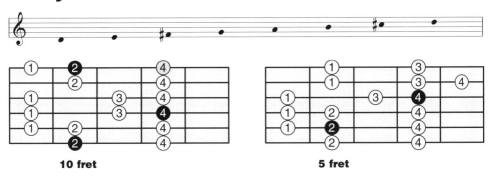

10 fret **5 fret**

D natural minor

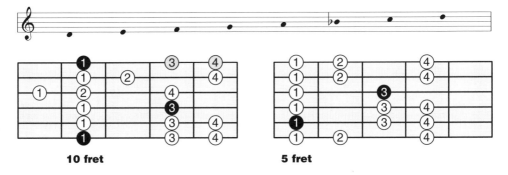

10 fret **5 fret**

D melodic minor

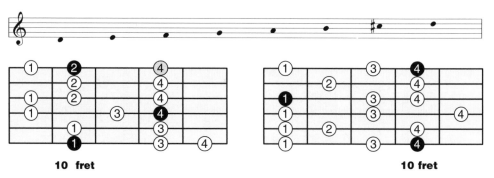

D harmonic minor

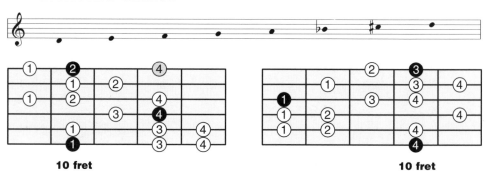

D dorian

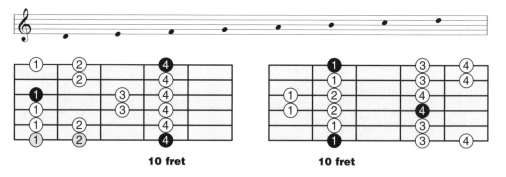

D mixolydian

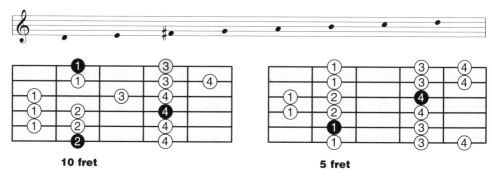

10 fret   5 fret

D whole tone

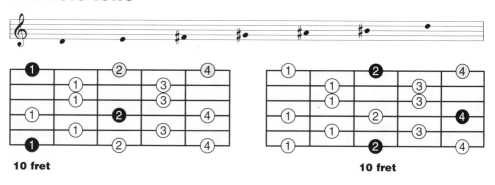

10 fret   10 fret

D diminished

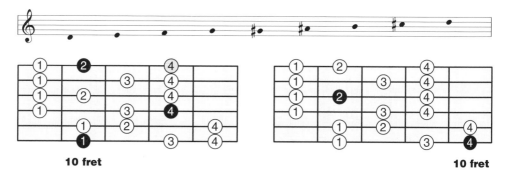

10 fret   10 fret

E♭ (D♯) Scales

E♭ minor pentatonic

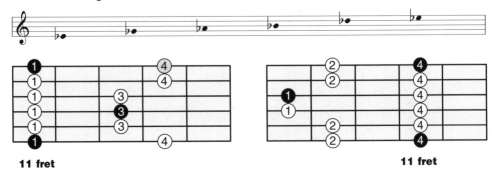

11 fret

11 fret

E♭ major pentatonic

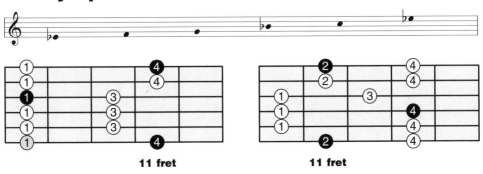

11 fret

11 fret

E♭ blues scale

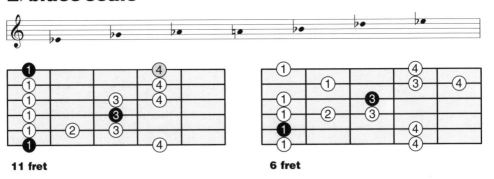

11 fret

6 fret

E♭ country scale

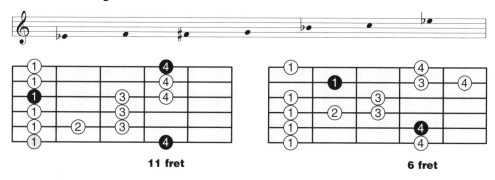

11 fret   **6 fret**

E♭ major

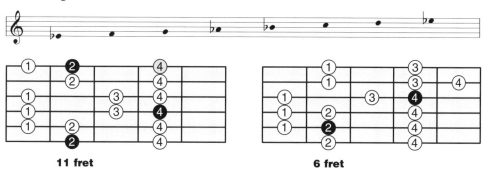

11 fret   **6 fret**

E♭ natural minor

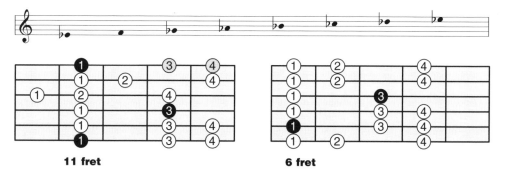

11 fret   **6 fret**

E♭ melodic minor

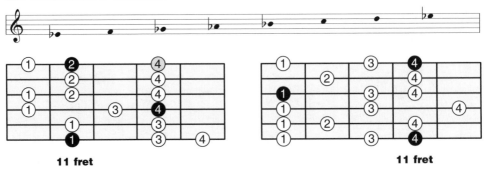

11 fret   11 fret

E♭ harmonic minor

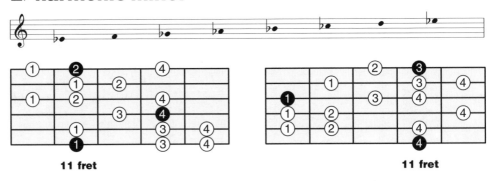

11 fret   11 fret

E♭ dorian

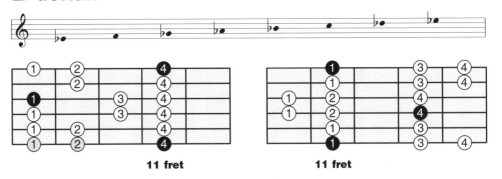

11 fret   11 fret

Eb mixolydian

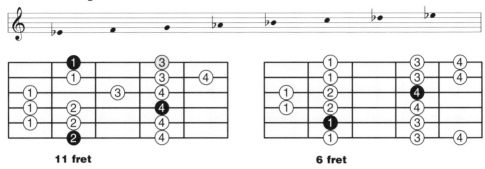

Eb whole tone

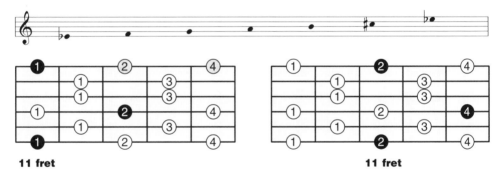

Eb diminished

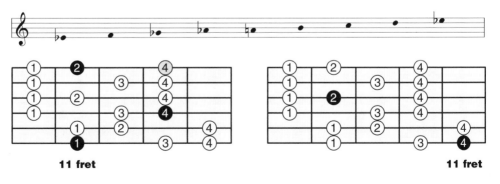

E Scales

E minor pentatonic

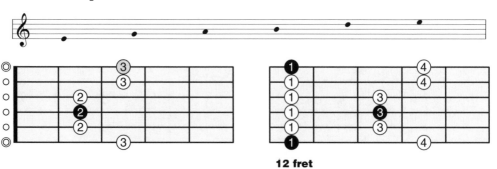

12 fret

E major pentatonic

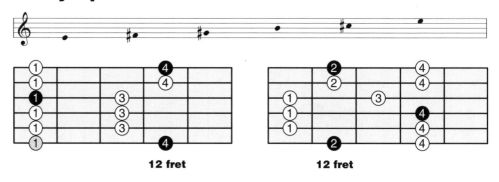

12 fret   **12 fret**

E blues scale

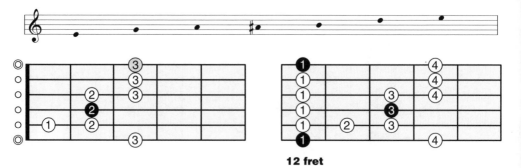

12 fret

E Scales

E country scale

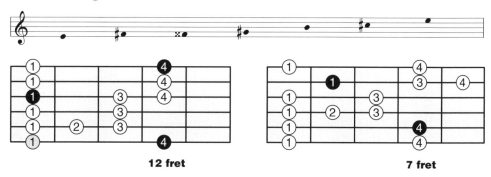

12 fret

7 fret

E major

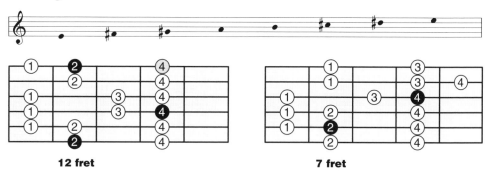

12 fret

7 fret

E natural minor

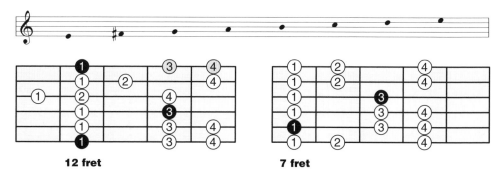

12 fret

7 fret

E Scales

E melodic minor

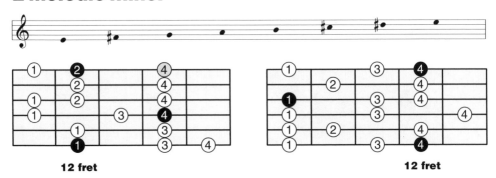

E harmonic minor

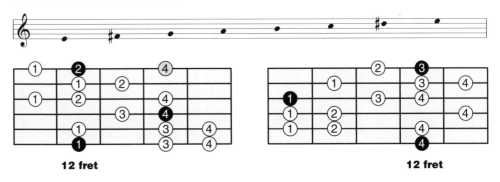

E dorian

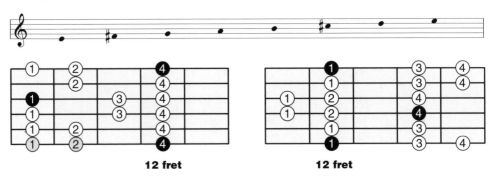

32

12 fret

12 fret

12 fret

12 fret

12 fret

12 fret

E mixolydian

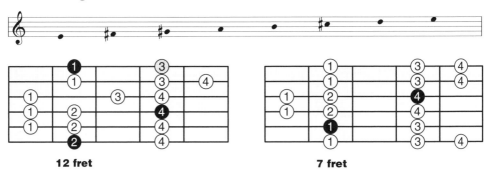

12 fret   **7 fret**

E whole tone

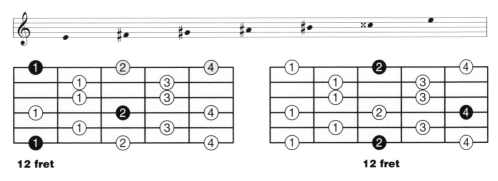

12 fret   **12 fret**

E diminished

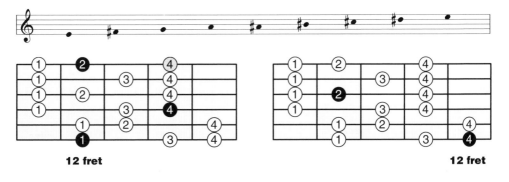

12 fret   **12 fret**

F Scales

F minor pentatonic

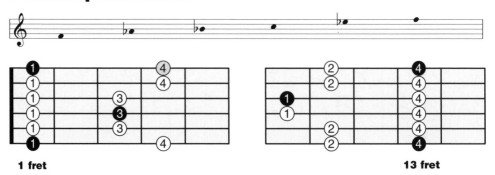

1 fret · 13 fret

F major pentatonic

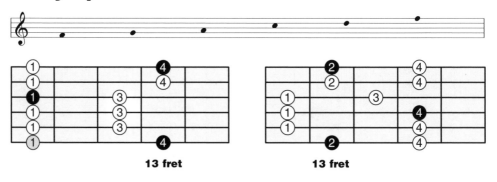

13 fret · 13 fret

F blues scale

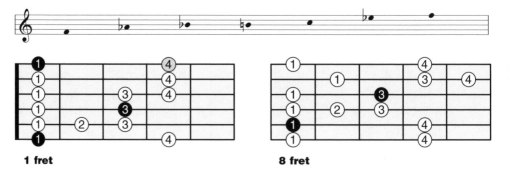

1 fret · 8 fret

F country scale

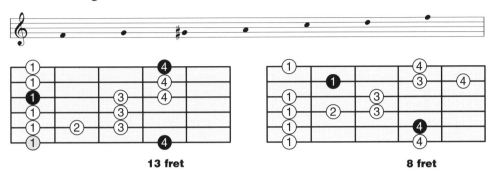

13 fret   8 fret

F major

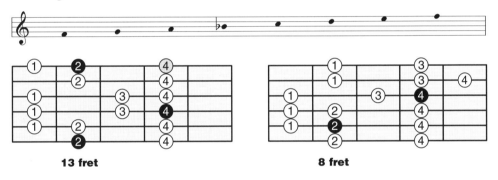

13 fret   8 fret

F natural minor

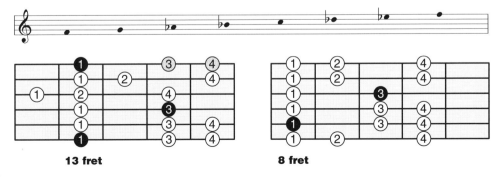

13 fret   8 fret

F melodic minor

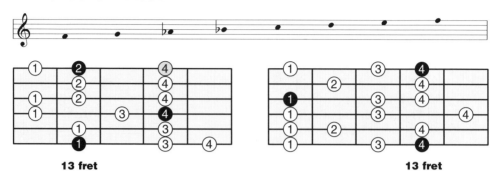

F harmonic minor

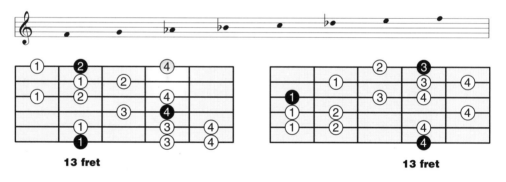

F dorian

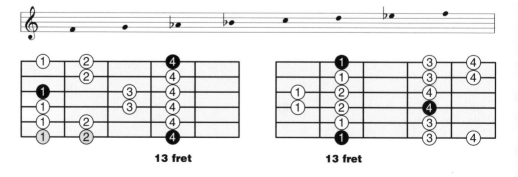

F mixolydian

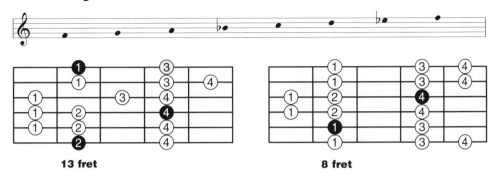

13 fret

8 fret

F whole tone

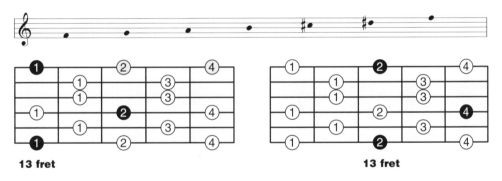

13 fret

13 fret

F diminished

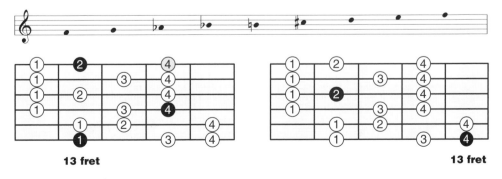

13 fret

13 fret

F♯ (G♭) Scales

F♯ minor pentatonic

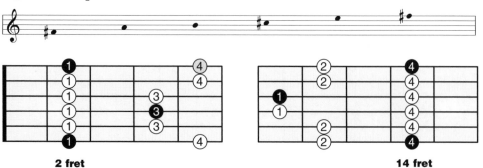

2 fret   14 fret

F♯ major pentatonic

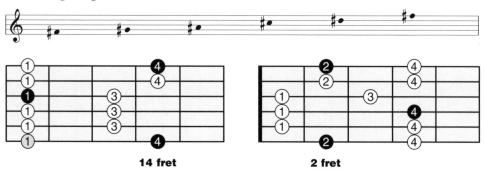

14 fret   2 fret

F♯ blues scale

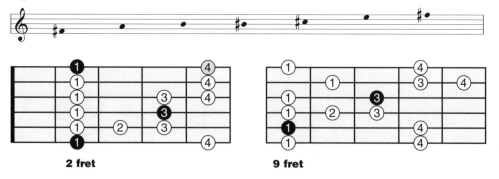

2 fret   9 fret

F♯ country scale

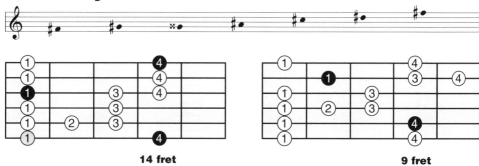

14 fret

9 fret

F♯ major

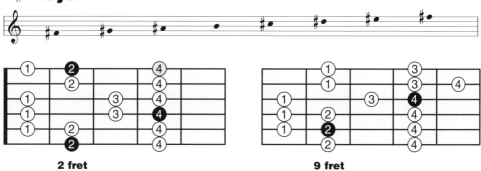

2 fret

9 fret

F♯ natural minor

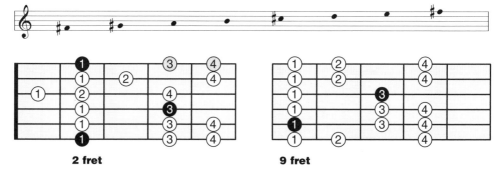

2 fret

9 fret

F♯ melodic minor

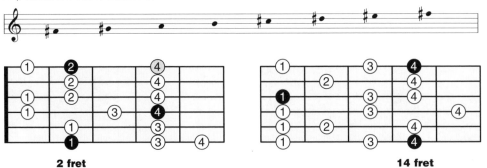

2 fret — 14 fret

F♯ harmonic minor

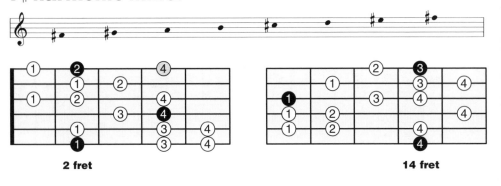

2 fret — 14 fret

F♯ dorian

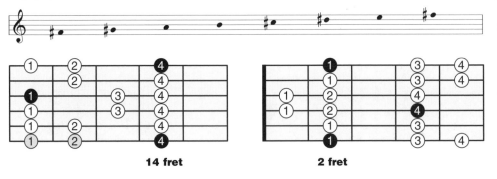

14 fret — 2 fret

F♯ mixolydian

2 fret   9 fret

F♯ whole tone

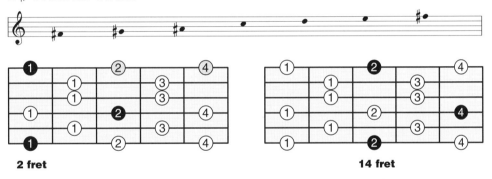

2 fret   14 fret

F♯ diminished

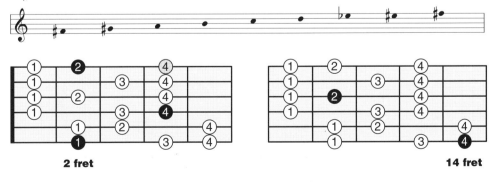

2 fret   14 fret

G Scales

G minor pentatonic

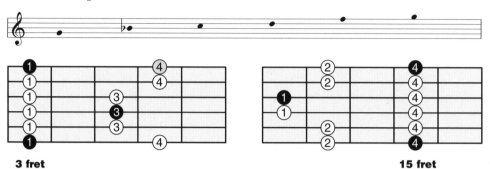

3 fret

15 fret

G major pentatonic

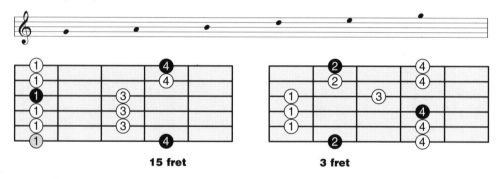

15 fret

3 fret

G blues scale

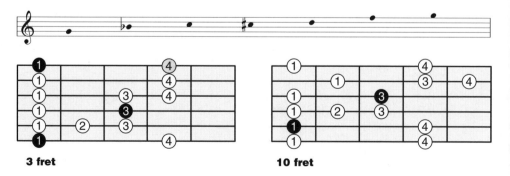

3 fret

10 fret

G Scales

G country scale

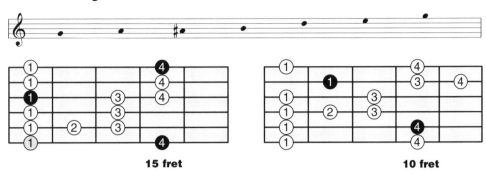

15 fret   **10 fret**

G major

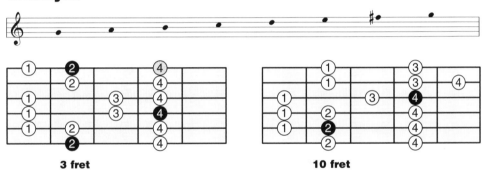

3 fret   **10 fret**

G natural minor

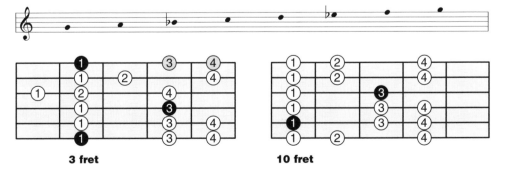

3 fret   **10 fret**

G Scales

G melodic minor

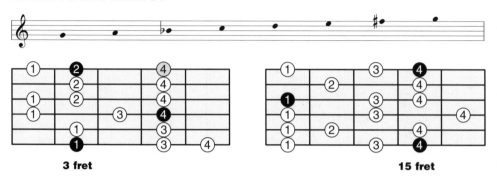

3 fret

15 fret

G harmonic minor

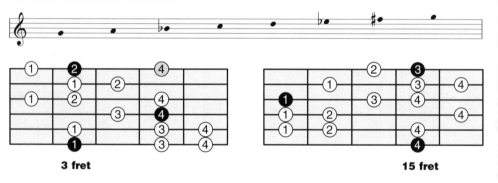

3 fret

15 fret

G dorian

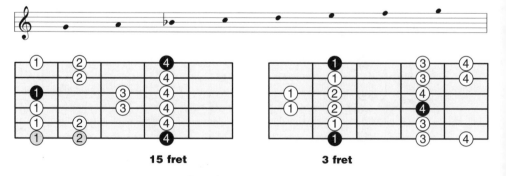

15 fret

3 fret

G Scales

G mixolydian

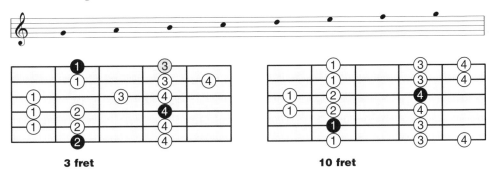

3 fret · 10 fret

G whole tone

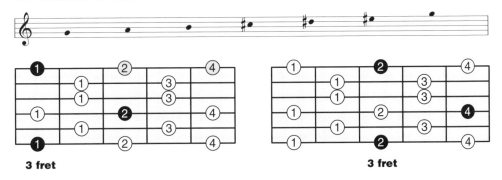

3 fret · 3 fret

G diminished

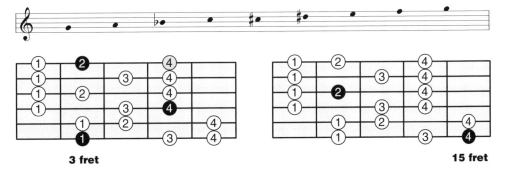

3 fret · 15 fret

49

A♭ (G♯) Scales

A♭ minor pentatonic

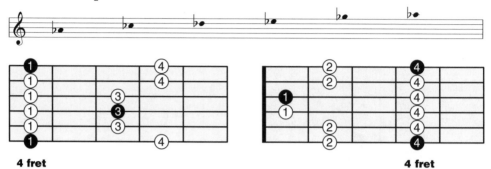

4 fret   4 fret

A♭ major pentatonic

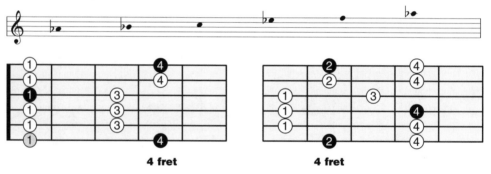

4 fret   4 fret

A♭ blues scale

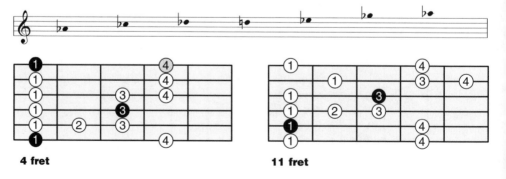

4 fret   11 fret

A♭ (G♯) Scales

A♭ country scale

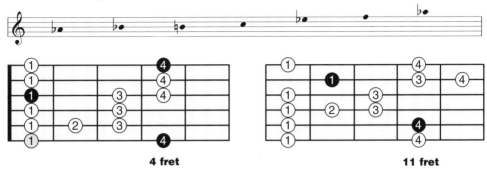

A♭ major

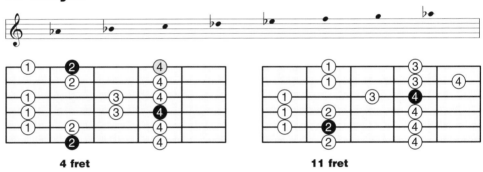

A♭ natural minor

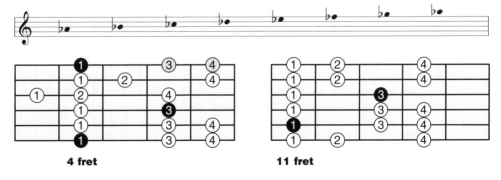

Ab melodic minor

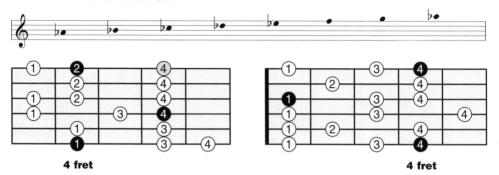

4 fret   4 fret

Ab harmonic minor

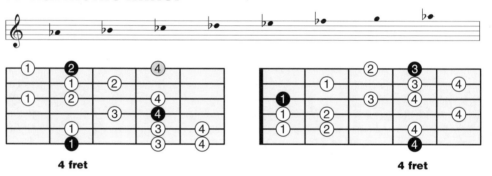

4 fret   4 fret

Ab dorian

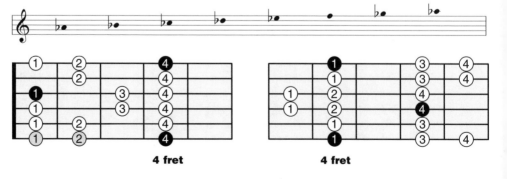

4 fret   4 fret

Ab mixolydian

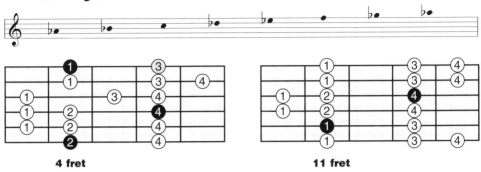

4 fret   11 fret

Ab whole tone

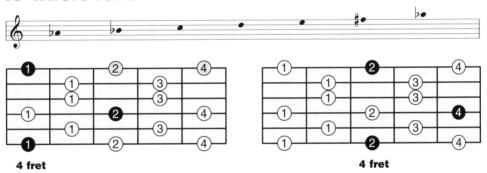

4 fret   4 fret

Ab diminished

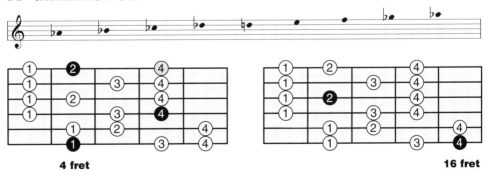

4 fret   16 fret

More Scales

Although this book shows you how to play all of the most popular scales in every key, there are in fact hundreds, even thousands, of other scales that you can play on the guitar.

Most of them are exotic scales that are normally only used in modern jazz, contemporary classical music or folk tunes from Asian, Eastern European and African countries, but each one has a distinctive sound and you might be able to use some of them to add a little bit of extra spice to your music!

All of the scales shown below are from a root note of C. The Spanish and Hungarian ones are often played in European gypsy music, while the Indian scale is a pentatonic that usually turns up in Indian classical and pop music. The Neapolitan and Javanese scales are even more exotic. Play around with these - and as many other scales as you can find - and see what you can come up with. You may be surprised!

Spanish

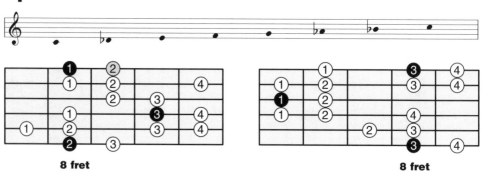

Hungarian

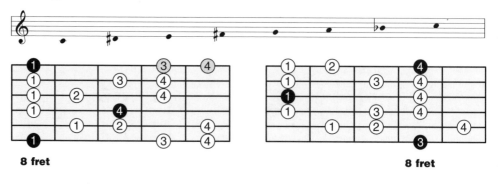

More Scales

52 Indian

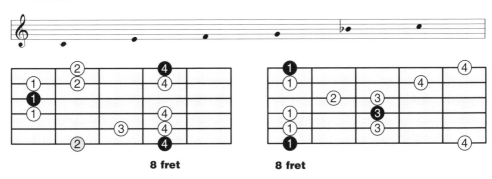

8 fret   **8 fret**

53 Neapolitan

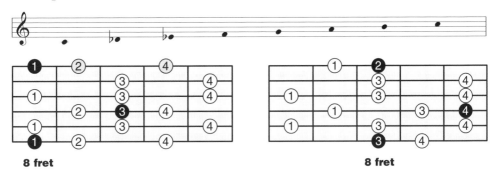

8 fret   **8 fret**

54 Javanese

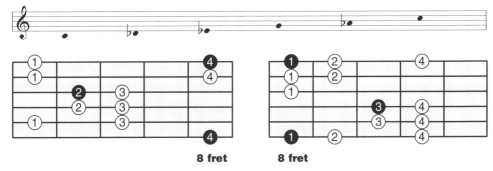

8 fret   **8 fret**

Further Reading

IF YOU'VE ENJOYED this book and are now looking for some songs to play, here's a sample of just some of the great **Really Easy Guitar!** titles available from Music Sales. You can order these from your local music or book shop, or in case of difficulty, check out the 'tutor zone' at **www.musicsales.com**.

Each of the books in the Really Easy Guitar series contains songs arranged in the easy-to-follow 'chords and lyrics' style, with full 'soundalike' backing tracks to play along to! There are also hints and tips for each song, and excerpts of TAB for the famous riffs or intros that you've always wanted to learn. Everything you need to know to play your favourite songs!

The Beatles NO90692

Includes: 'Day Tripper', 'Help!', 'Here Comes The Sun', 'While My Guitar Gently Weeps' and 10 other top Beatles hits.

Rock Classics AM957693

Includes: 'All Along The Watchtower' – Jimi Hendrix, 'All Right Now' – Free, 'Message In A Bottle' – The Police, 'The Boys Are Back In Town' – Thin Lizzy and 10 other Rock-tastic tunes!

90s Hits AM957715

Includes: 'Animal Nitrate' – Suede, 'Disco 2000' – Pulp, 'Wild Wood' – Paul Weller, along with 10 other '90s Indie-Rock classics!

Bob Dylan AM971828

Includes: 'Like A Rolling Stone', 'Lay Lady Lay', 'Just Like A Woman', and 9 more Bob Dylan strum-along favourites.

21st Century Rock AM975645

Includes 'Bohemian Like You' – The Dandy Warhols, 'Plug In Baby' – Muse, 'Vegas Two Times' – Stereophonics, 'Yellow' – Coldplay and 8 more new rock hits.

Bryan Adams AM971806

Includes: 'Run To You', 'Summer Of '69', '18 Till I Die', 'When You're Gone' and 8 more Bryan Adams hits.

Chords AM969683

Includes a wide selection of chords in all of the popular keys. An essential reference book for all guitar players!

To remove your CD from the plastic sleeve, lift the small lip on the right to break the perforated flap. Replace the disc after use for convenient storage.